paper fun!

Projects to fold, bend, cut, and curl!

by Patricia Doherty

✪ American Girl™

Questions or comments? Call 1-800-845-0005,
visit our Web site at **americangirl.com**,
or write to Customer Service, American Girl,
8400 Fairway Place, Middleton, WI 53562-0497.

Printed in China

06 07 08 09 10 11 LEO 10 9 8 7 6 5 4 3 2 1

American Girl™ and its associated logos are trademarks of American Girl, LLC.

Editorial Development: Trula Magruder

Art Direction and Design: Camela Decaire, Chris David

Production: Jeannette Bailey, Judith Lary, Mindy Rappe, and Kendra Schluter

Photography: Radlund Photography

Stylist: Patricia Doherty

Dear Reader,

Wear quilled paper earrings to a party.
Watch tissue-paper fish float in your room.
Inside this book, you'll discover dozens of
ways to play with paper. Tons of tips, fun
crafting supplies, pretty paper, and easy
instructions will give you the inspiration
you need to brighten a room, transform
your style, or create a treasured gift. So
get started, and paper your world!

Your friends at American Girl

contents

rip it up

cut it out

fold it up

wrap and roll it

rip it up

Piece together torn strips of paper for cool collage crafts.

Getting Started

Paper

To collage, you'll need to tear a lot of paper strips! Try different sizes of strips and experiment with all kinds of paper, such as candy wrappers or paper bags.

Mod Podge

We used Mod Podge to make our crafts—it's a glue with a sealant in it—but white glue mixed with a little water will work for most projects. Use a paintbrush or your fingers to apply Mod Podge to paper strips. Overlap strips so that you don't leave gaps. For a bowl, start at the bottom and work to the top. Make two layers.

Work Area

Mod Podge gets really messy, so always keep your work table covered with wax paper, and keep a wet washcloth nearby for drips and spills.

Drying Times

We've given our drying times, but since you may use more Mod Podge or have a cooler room than we did, your project could still be damp. If that happens, flip it upside down to dry a few hours more.

Double-Stick Tape

We use double-stick tape because it's sticky on both sides, so paper lies flatter. You'll find double-stick tape at office-supply, scrapbooking, and craft stores. If you prefer to use glue, apply it with a toothpick so that you're using a tiny dab at a time.

flying fish

You don't need an aquarium to watch these fish float by!

1. Cover work area. Lay a 12-by-12-inch square of wax paper on top. Tear tissue paper into strips. Lay a strip on the wax paper square, and brush it with Mod Podge.

2. Overlap second strip with first one. Coat with more Mod Podge. Keep mixing paper colors until you cover all of wax paper square. Let dry overnight.

3. Peel wax paper from tissue sheet. Trace fish stencils over tissue sheet, then cut out fish.

4. Tape fishing line to each fish. To hide tape, press scrap tissue over it. Hang fish by a window.

bright bowl

Create a pretty bowl for candies, trinkets, or office supplies.

in your kit:
• colored paper

you will need:
• wax paper
• Mod Podge
• tiny dish
• small glass bowl
• plastic wrap
• scissors

Tip: For larger projects, you may not have enough paper in your kit. If this happens, use a coordinating paper.

1. Cover work area with wax paper. Tear colored paper into strips. Pour Mod Podge into tiny dish. Press plastic wrap inside glass bowl, smoothing out wrinkles and air bubbles.

2. Dip fingers into Mod Podge and rub front and back of paper strip. Press strip into bottom of bowl.

3. Overlap next strip, working from bottom center out. Repeat with a second layer. Smooth out paper wrinkles. Let dry 24 hours.

4. Pull up on plastic wrap to remove paper bowl from glass bowl. Peel wrap from paper bowl. Trim edges even with scissors, if desired.

Tip: Experiment with paper! Add cutout paper shapes, try patterned paper, or use candy wrappers.

11

mini masterpiece
Create a necklace that's a work of art!

in your kit:
- tissue paper
- colored paper
- picture pebble

you will need:
- wax paper
- paintbrush
- tiny dish
- Mod Podge
- white craft paper
- scissors
- embroidery floss
- double-stick tape

1. Cover work area. To make a background, brush tissue strip with Mod Podge. Lay strip on white craft paper. Layer more strips to cover small area on paper.

2. Cut a shape from tissue or colored paper. Brush Mod Podge over back of shape and press it to background. (Or leave background plain.) Let dry.

3. Peel backing from picture pebble. Press pebble over design. Trim off extra paper.

4. Fold a piece of floss in half. Tape center of it to back. Cover tape and floss with scrap paper. Tie necklace on yourself.

jewelry bowl

Dangle earrings around the edge of a dainty dish.

in your kit:
• colored paper

you will need:
• wax paper
• Mod Podge
• tiny dish
• soup bowl with lip
• plastic wrap
• pencil
• scissors
• hole punch

1. Cover work area. Follow steps 1 through 3 from page 10, but extend paper over soup bowl lip as shown. Then follow step 4.

2. Draw a wave pattern around bowl and cut it out. Punch pairs of holes as shown below. Fill bowl with jewelry and hang earrings from holes.

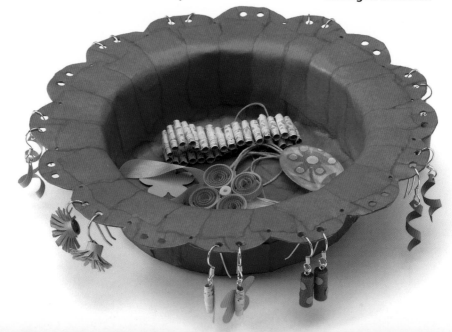

hair-band bloom

Put petals on ponytails with a crafty hair band.

in your kit:
- wide quilling paper
- flower brad

you will need:
- wax paper
- paintbrush
- tiny dish
- Mod Podge
- micro hole punch
  (see "Hole Punches,"
  page 16)
- double-stick tape
- hair elastic

1. Cover work area. Cut quilling paper into eight $2\frac{3}{4}$-inch-long strips. Brush Mod Podge on one side of each strip. Let dry on clean wax paper.

2. With the Mod Podge side facing out, bend a strip in half—do not crease! Holding ends even, punch a hole through both ends. Slip on flower brad post. Repeat with 7 remaining strips.

3. Open brad until it's completely flat to hold petals. Wrap a small piece of tape around a hair elastic. Stick elastic to back of brad.

4. Cut a $1\frac{1}{4}$-inch quilling strip. Brush Mod Podge on one side. Press wet side down over elastic and onto flower. Let dry.

Tip: Make a hair band in school colors!

cut it out

Shape up your paper projects with punches.

Getting Started

Hole Punches

A micro punch has a smaller hole than a regular hole punch (see below). You can find one almost anywhere craft and paper supplies are sold. If you can't get a micro hole punch, ask a parent to help you make tiny holes with a pushpin or tack.

Punch Catch

⭐ A punch catch is the hinged flap that catches paper after you punch a hole. If you want to put a punch in an exact spot, ask an adult to help you remove the catch.

Hole Reinforcements

You can find hole reinforcements at office and craft stores. If you don't have any, but you have a small round sticker, punch a hole in the center of it with a hole punch.

Beading Cord

Beading cord is stretchy, so you can slip it on and off. That makes it slippery, too. To make a knot permanent, dab craft glue on the knot and let it dry. You'll find extra beading cord at craft stores.

Note: Always have an adult help you where you see this hand ⭐ or when you think something sounds a bit hard for you to do alone.

17

punch jewelry

Put paper punches to work making perfect jewelry pieces.

in your kit:
- card stock
- beading cord

you will need:
- flower punch
- micro hole punch
- craft glue

Punch out flowers from card stock. In the center of each flower, punch 2 holes, spaced apart. Thread beading cord through the flowers, then slide them into position along the cord. Cut the cord to fit on your neck or wrist. To secure it, tie a double knot in the ends, then dab craft glue onto the knot. Let dry.

Tip: Try a larger or smaller flower punch, then tape the flowers together before punching beading holes.

i.d. tag

Create a dazzling designer tag for a tote, purse, or pack.

in your kit:
- foil paper
- card stock

you will need:
- glue
- fun font
- pencil
- scissors
- hole punch
- ball chain or ribbon

Glue foil paper to card stock. Find a large letter in a magazine or from a computer font. Cut out the letter you like, then trace around it onto the card stock. Cut out the traced letter. Punch a hole in the corner of the letter, slide on a chain or ribbon, and attach it to a zipper.

19

mod mobile

Put a spin on an old space with a mobile.

in your kit:
- flower stencils
- card stock
- vellum

you will need:
- pencil
- scissors
- large circle punch
- double-stick tape
- embroidery floss

Trace the large flower stencil onto card stock, and cut out the flower. Trace the small flower stencil onto vellum, and cut out the flower. Tape one vellum flower to each card flower. Punch or cut out circles, and tape one to each flower center. Tape a strand of floss onto the back of each flower. To hide the tape, press scrap paper over the sticky tape. Make more flowers. Hang mobile in your room.

picnic chicks

Gather your girlfriends for a chicks picnic party!

in your kit:
- colored paper

you will need:
- colorful paper cups, plates, and napkins
- hole reinforcements
- markers and gel pens
- scissors
- hole punch
- ribbon

Use hole reinforcements to design chicks on picnic supplies—keep the stickers away from the cup edges and centers of plates. Add beaks, eyes, and feet with markers or gel pens.

For a napkin ring, cut a paper strip. Decorate with chicks. Punch a hole through each end, then tie the strip closed with a ribbon.

21

spray sachets

Spritz fragrance on paper cutouts for scented closets and drawers.

in your kit:
• large flower stencil
• card stock

you will need:
• pencil
• scissors
• paper punch
• ribbon
• wax paper
• fragrance

Trace the large flower stencil onto card stock, and cut it out. Try squares and other shapes, too! Punch a hole at the top of each cutout. Thread on a ribbon, and tie the ribbon into a bow. Lay the cutouts on wax paper, then spritz lightly with fragrance. Let dry. Hang in a closet or place in a dresser drawer.

dinky daisies

To brighten someone's day, punch out a bitty bouquet.

in your kit:
- colored paper or vellum

you will need:
- tiny flower paper punch
- hole punch
- double-stick tape
- scissors
- green jewelry wire
- tiny bottle or jar

Punch out a flower and a circle from paper or vellum. Tape the circle to the flower.

★ Ask an adult to help you cut wire for a stem. At one end of the wire, make a small bend. Tape the bend underneath the flower. Make more flowers, and slip them into a tiny bottle or jar for a vase.

Tip: Keep stems straight or curl them around a pencil.

fold it up

Bend and fold paper into pretty pieces of art.

Getting Started

Wrapping

To wrap around a flat object, measure and cut your paper so that it's only a few inches wider on all sides than the object to wrap. Place the object in the center of your paper. Cut out the corners as shown. Fold in opposite ends, and tape down. Then fold and tape the other sides.

Professional Finish

For a professional look, take extra time to line up all your edges so that they're perfectly even before you fold them, don't use too much glue, and be willing to remake a craft if it's not exactly the way you want it.

Tape Measure

The tape measure in your kit has two uses: 1) to measure lengths, and 2) to help you evenly place the holes you want to punch out. To do this, lay the tape measure near where you want your holes to be, then make a dot below each of the circles on the tape. Now place your punch over each dot and punch.

fan file

Display photos, cards, and art in this file.

1. Cut ten 6-by-3-inch pieces of card stock. Lay tape along narrow end of each piece, line edges perfectly together, then bend to make a flap—do not crease.

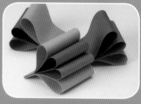

2. Tape 3 flaps together at bottom edges as shown. Set aside. Repeat with 3 more flaps, and again with 4 flaps.

3. Tape all 3 groups of flaps together. Keep group of 4 flaps in the middle.

4. Roll four 24-inch strips of quilling paper into pegs and glue closed (see page 34). Glue on pegs.

earring wave

Give earrings a ride on a wacky earring holder.

in your kit:
- pretty paper
- card stock
- tape measure

you will need:
- cardboard rectangle
- scissors
- double-stick tape
- pencil
- micro hole punch
- 4 adhesive pop dots
  (sold at craft stores)
- adhesive wall hanger
  or magnetic strip

1. Cover cardboard front with tape, then wrap with paper (see page 24). Cut a card-stock strip longer than cardboard. Use tape measure to mark dots along bottom of card strip. Punch holes over dots (see page 24).

2. Space and place pop dots evenly along center of cardboard. Press end of punched strip onto first pop dot. Bend paper into a small wave, then press onto next dot. Repeat for each dot. Trim extra paper. Hang.

love light

Turn on this lamp for a little glow.

you will need:
- tape measure
- rice paper and/or card stock
- scissors
- double-stick tape
- push light

Measure around a push light, then measure and cut your paper length so that it's one inch longer. Lay the paper shade flat to tape paper shapes onto it, if desired. Press a strip of tape along the vertical edge of the shade, then bend the shade back around the push light to tape closed.

Tip: Look for push lights at home-supply and discount stores.

coin purse

Keep coins, cards, or candy in this petite purse.

1. Lay bag with flap side up. Draw a line across bag 2¼ inches from flap, then cut off top.

2. Open bag and lightly draw a line along fold to make a large triangle on each side, as shown.

3. Cut down side edge of bag to triangle. Cut off side, leaving triangle as shown. Repeat for opposite side.

4. Cut off front of bag, leaving a tiny edge. Fold and decorate. Slip bag under a heavy book until bag lies flat.

Tip: Try scalloped, fringed, or straight edges decorated with ribbon, markers, stickers, or punched shapes.

locker frame

Find 1-2-3 fun ways to use a locker frame.

in your kit:
- pretty paper

you will need:
- scissors
- thick cardboard or art board
- ¼-inch-wide flat elastic
- stapler
- glue
- heavy adhesive magnetic strip

1. Cover a cardboard rectangle with colored paper (see page 24). Tightly wrap elastic around rectangle so that it overlaps itself. Slide elastic off board.

2. Staple overlap of elastic, trim it, and slide it back onto frame. Repeat with one or more elastic pieces as shown at right. Press magnetic strip on back of cardboard. Slip in flowers, a photo, or a mirror.

wrap and roll it

Curl quilling paper into easy earrings and more.

Getting Started

How to Quill a Shape

1. Slip a quilling paper strip into quilling tool slot.

2. Tightly roll paper to end of strip.

3. Pull out tool, and glue paper end closed. You may need to push layers back into a roll shape.

4. If you want a tight coil, hold paper tightly until you glue end closed. If you want a loose coil, let paper go, then glue closed.

How to Roll a Bead

1. Trace bead stencil onto paper and cut out shape.

3. Remove skewer. Glue end of paper closed, holding it a few seconds until dry.

2. Beginning with wide end, roll triangle tightly around a skewer or knitting needle.

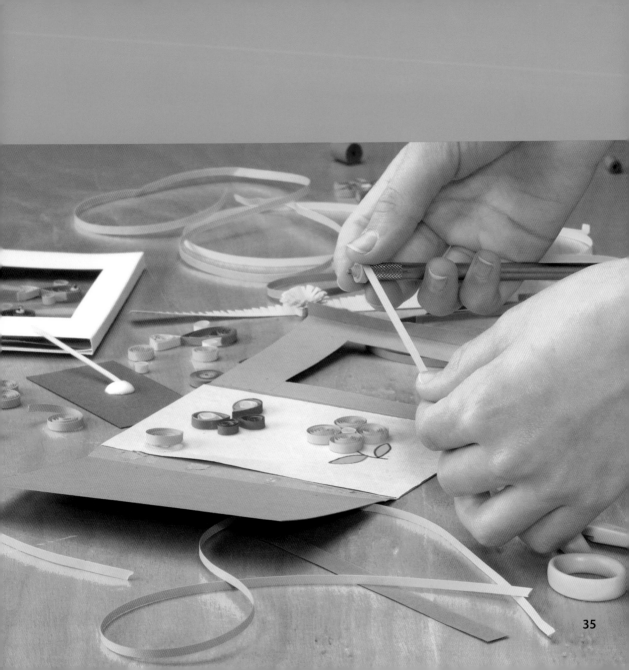

quilled creations

Curl paper to create lots of artsy creatures.

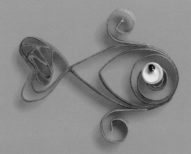

swishing fish

For a fish body, roll a 6-inch strip of narrow quilling paper into a loose coil. Glue the end closed (see page 34). For a tail, roll a 4-inch strip. Pinch one end of coil to make a point, and press in the other end. For fins, roll two 1-inch strips halfway. Glue the pieces together as shown. Glue on a googly eye.

swirling flower

Roll a 6-inch strip of narrow quilling paper into a tight peg, then glue the end closed. Set aside. For a petal, roll a 12-inch paper strip into a loose coil (see page 34), then glue the end closed. Repeat with 3 more petals. Glue the petals around the peg.

soaring butterfly
Roll a 2-inch strip of
wide quilling paper and
a 6-inch strip of narrow
quilling paper into pegs.
For a big wing, glue three
2-inch strips of narrow
quilling paper (in 3 different colors) into a long line.
Roll the first color tighter
than the other two. Pinch
wing into a teardrop. For
small wing, repeat using
two 1 1/2-inch strips. Glue
pieces together as shown.

quilled card

Create an inspiring art card.

in your kit:
- window card
- colored paper

you will need:
- ruler
- 2 toothpicks
- double-stick tape
- quilled creations
  (pages 36–37)
- craft glue
- colored pencils or
  markers

1. Lay a ruler along white score line of window card. Run a toothpick along ruler, to "draw" a crease in card. Repeat at each white line. Fold at creases.

2. Tape paper onto center flap. Use toothpick to dab glue onto quilled creations, and stick them to paper. Draw on other accents.

3. Run glue along flap edge, then fold and stick it to the left spine. Stand card up to display it.

jazzy jewelry

Turn quilled creations into clever jewelry.

in your kit:
- **quilling tool**
- **narrow quilling paper**
- **beading cord**

you will need:
- **craft glue**
- **quilled creations (pages 36–37)**
- **ribbon**
- **double-stick tape**

Roll a 1-inch strip of narrow quilling paper into a tight peg, and glue closed. Glue the peg to the back of a quilled creation. Slide beading cord through the center of the peg, and tie cord around your neck.

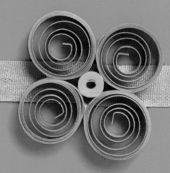

Tip: Tape a quilled flower to a ribbon. Tie the ribbon around your wrist.

fringe flower earrings

Be a petal pusher with pretty paper earrings.

in your kit:
- wide quilling paper
- narrow quilling paper
- quilling tool
- earring hooks

you will need:
- scissors
- glue

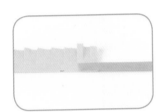

1. For each earring, glue a 6-inch strip of wide quilling paper to end of a 6-inch strip of narrow quilling paper. Cut a fringe along wide strip.

2. Starting at narrow end, slip strip end into slot on quilling tool. Roll strip into a peg—keep fringed end facing up. Remove tool. Glue paper end closed. Fluff fringe.

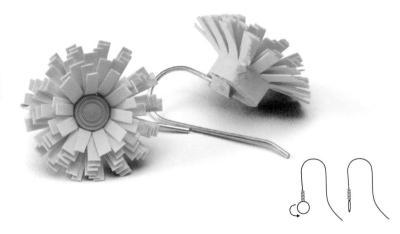

3. Twist earring hook to get end to lie flat against flower (see illustration at left). Glue hook to a small piece of quilling paper, then glue hook and paper to flower.

beauty beads

Design jewelry for any event, outfit, or season.

in your kit:
- bead stencil
- pretty paper
- beading cord
- eye pins
- earring hooks

you will need:
- wooden skewer
- craft glue
- scissors

1. For a bracelet, trace bead stencil onto pretty paper. Roll about 18 beads (see page 34). Cut 4 feet of beading cord. String one bead onto middle of cord.

2. For a second bead, stick right end of cord into right side of bead, then pull through. Insert left end of cord into left side of same bead, then pull through (see illustration below). Pull ends tight.

3. Repeat step 2 for each bead. To finish, pull end of cord through first bead once and tie tightly a few times. Trim extra cord. Dab knot with glue.

Tip: For bead earrings, roll 2 beads (see page 34). Put earring hooks on eye pins. Dab glue into ends of beads, then slip in eye pins. Let dry. For butterfly earrings, trace the wing stencil 2 times on paper, and cut out the wings. Glue each wing to a bead earring.

pretty pegs

Peg out! Design dozens of earrings in a mix of styles.

in your kit:
- wide quilling paper
- quilling tool
- eye pins
- earring hooks

you will need:
- scissors
- craft glue

For each earring, cut an $8^1/_2$-inch strip of wide quilling paper. Roll the strip into a peg (see page 34). Attach an eye pin to an earring hook. Dab glue into the end of the peg, then slip in the eye pin. Let dry. Leave plain, glue on paper-punched dots, or stick on gems.

 Tip: Eye pins in the kit are precut. If you buy more, ask an adult to cut them to $1/_2$ inch.

party fashion

Get your party started by creating a set of streamer earrings.

in your kit:
• narrow quilling paper
• earring hooks

you will need:
• scissors
• micro hole punch
  or pushpin
• skewer

For each earring, cut a 1½-inch strip of narrow quilling paper. Punch a small hole at the top of the strip. Attach an earring hook to the hole. Roll the strip loosely around a skewer.

good-night light

Decorate a plain shade with dangling beads.

in your kit:
- bead stencil
- colored paper

you will need:
- micro hole punch
  or pushpin
- paper lamp shade
- skewer
- glue
- eye pins
- hooks
- felt trim

Punch or poke holes where you
would like beads on a shade. Roll
as many beads as you'll need (see
page 34). For each bead, slip a
hook onto an eye pin. Dab glue
into the end of the bead, then
insert the eye pin. Let dry. Slip
the beads into the holes. Cover
holes with trim, if desired.

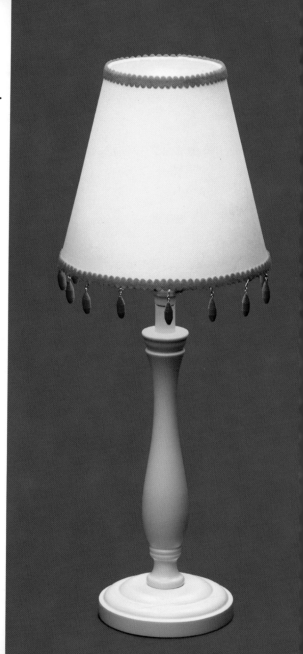